1000

STICKERS FOR BOYS

Pull out the sticker sheets and have them with you when you complete each page. There are also lots of extra stickers to use in this book or anywhere you like!

Designed by Katie Cox

make believe ideas

Dinosaur differences

Use your stickers to complete the scene.

Explore the island, then find and circle the 6 differences between the two pictures.

3

Dinosaur park

Match the stickers to the dino scene!

PARASAUROLOPHUS
Par-a-SORE-owe-loaf-uss

STEGOSAURUS
STEG-owe-SORE-uss

Shhhh . . . we are hiding in the cave!

Place some small dinosaurs here!

PTERODACTYL
Ter-owe-DAC-til

TRICERATOPS
Try-SERRA-tops

VELOCIRAPTOR
Vel-O-si-RAP-tor

SPINOSAURUS
Spy-no-SORE-uss

TYRANNOSAURUS REX
Tie-RAN-owe-SORE-uss-REX

Draw a crazy
dinosaur here!

6

Buried bones!

Find the 12 bones hidden in the dino scene.

T rex terror!

Copy and color the T rex, then add some sticker teeth and an eye!

8

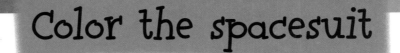

Then design
your own flag.

10

Get ready for liftoff!

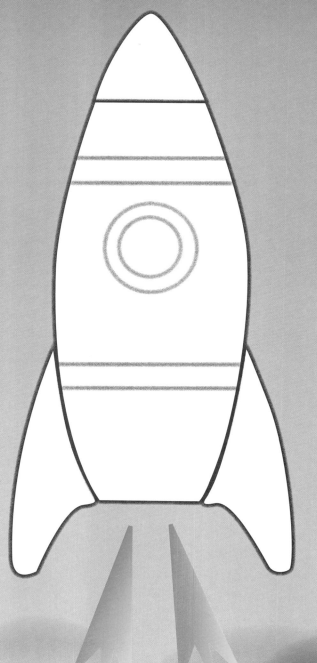

Use your stickers to complete the rocket and put some stars in the sky!

It's time to **explore** space!

Complete the scene with rockets, stars, and aliens!

13

Space race!

Sticker the space ships, then guess which one lands on the moon!

14

Space exploration

This is a new planet that has just been discovered. Add stickers and your own designs to make it an exciting place to visit!

beep!
beep!

glug!

boop!

Alien invaders!

Sticker 7 aliens onto the space station,
then guide the spaceman to his rocket.
Will he make it without meeting any aliens?

Start here!

Practice drawing spaceships here!

Fun fish!

Connect the dots to reveal
two big fun fish!

Color the fish and give them sticker eyes.

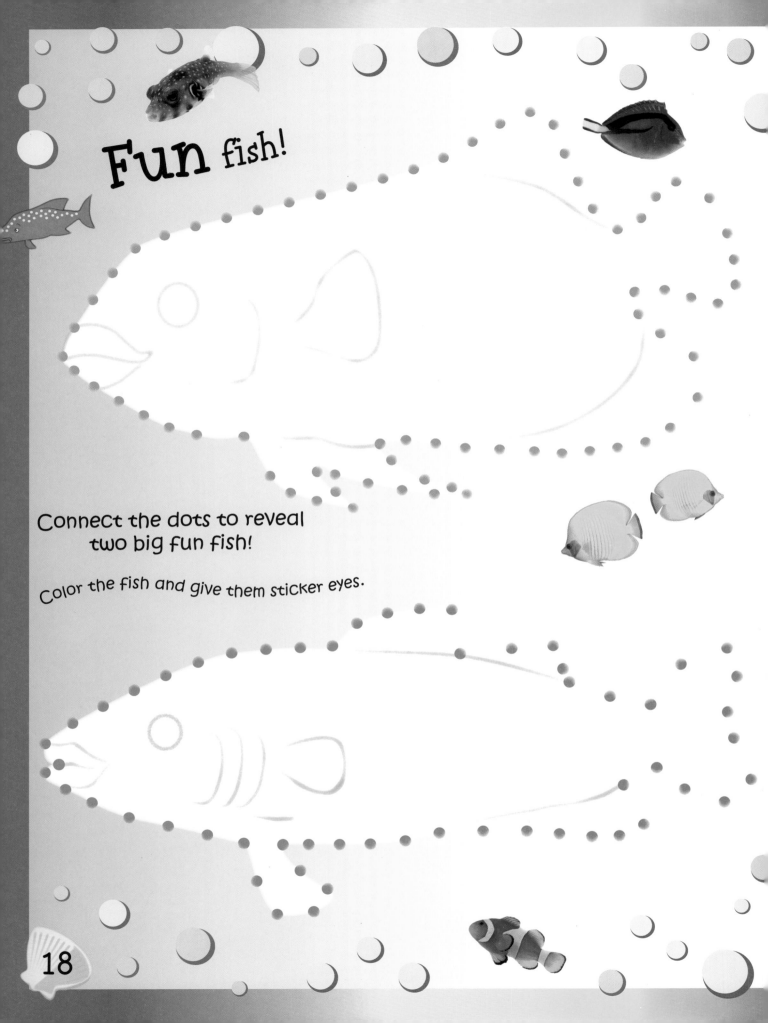

Fish hide-and-seek
Find stickers for the 8 hidden fish!

Help! Sharks!

19

Practice drawing sharks here!

Leaping dolphins!

Connect the dots and color the dolphins. Then add some sticker splashes!

Counting jellyfish!

Use your sticker answers to complete the jellyfish number puzzles!

How many jellyfish are there in each box?

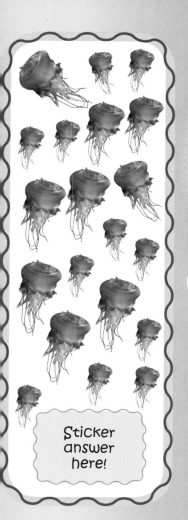

Sticker answer here!

Sticker answer here!

Sticker answer here!

23

Shark attack!

Fill the scene with fish and sharks!

Bug homes!

Find perfect homes for the bug stickers.

Picnic pests

Match the shapes with your stickers to find out who's eating the food at the picnic.

Add more bug stickers!

Find stickers to match the shapes!

Spider trap!

Draw a big spider at the end of the web, then match the stickers to find out who's been caught!

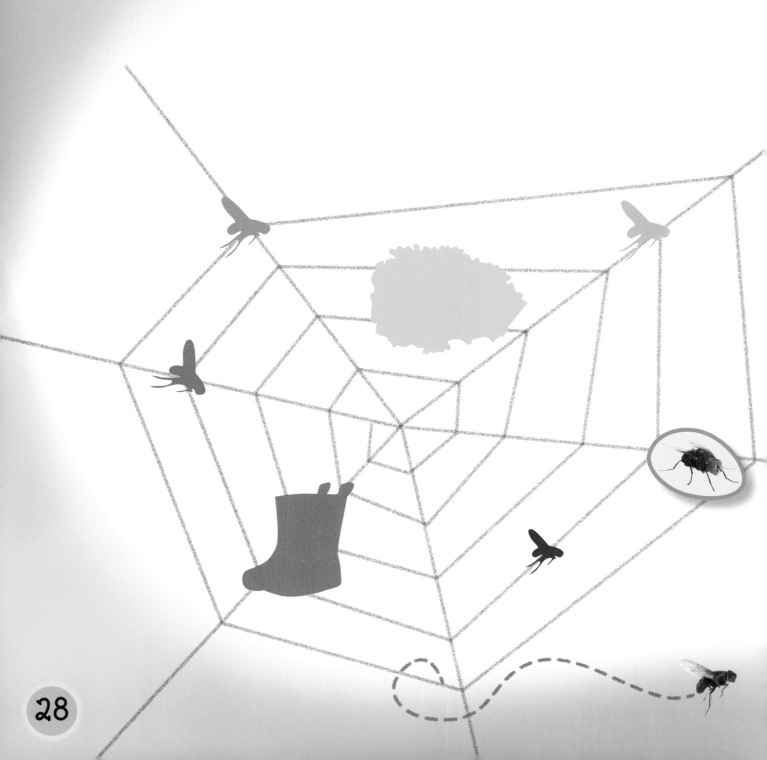

Design a bug!

We have given you its legs and its head— now you do the rest!

Find the ball!

Find stickers for the 8 sports balls.

30

Design your own sports gear here!

Use your favorite colors and patterns and add your team name.

Don't forget to add some stickers!

Ten-pin bowling

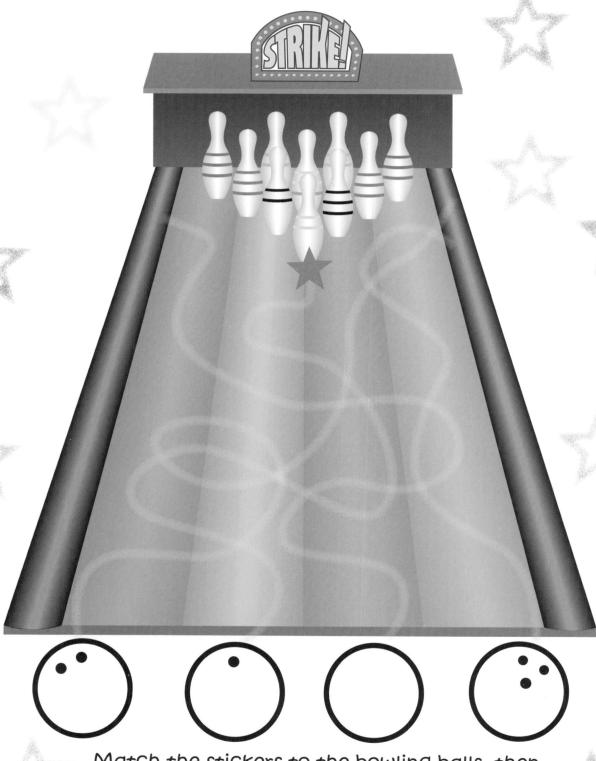

Match the stickers to the bowling balls, then guess which one scores a strike!

Olympic runners!

Become a sports star in this exciting race for two or more players!

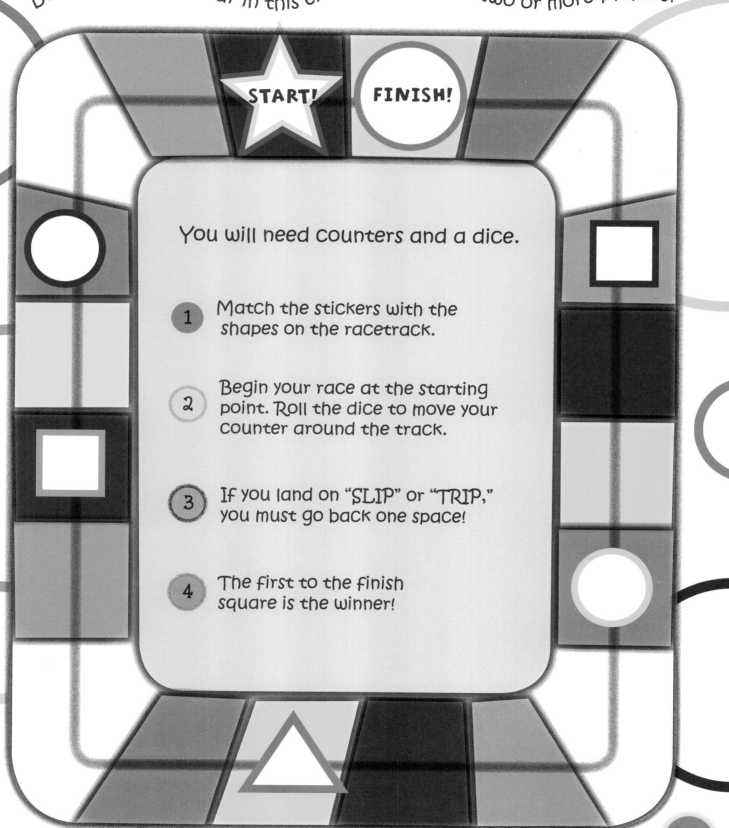

START!

FINISH!

You will need counters and a dice.

1. Match the stickers with the shapes on the racetrack.

2. Begin your race at the starting point. Roll the dice to move your counter around the track.

3. If you land on "SLIP" or "TRIP," you must go back one space!

4. The first to the finish square is the winner!

What can you see out of the window?

I can see 1 ....ar

I can see 2 ......gs

I can see 3 t.e.s

Find the missing stickers!

34

Get packing!

Find two stickers for each of the suitcases.

Things to wear

Things to eat

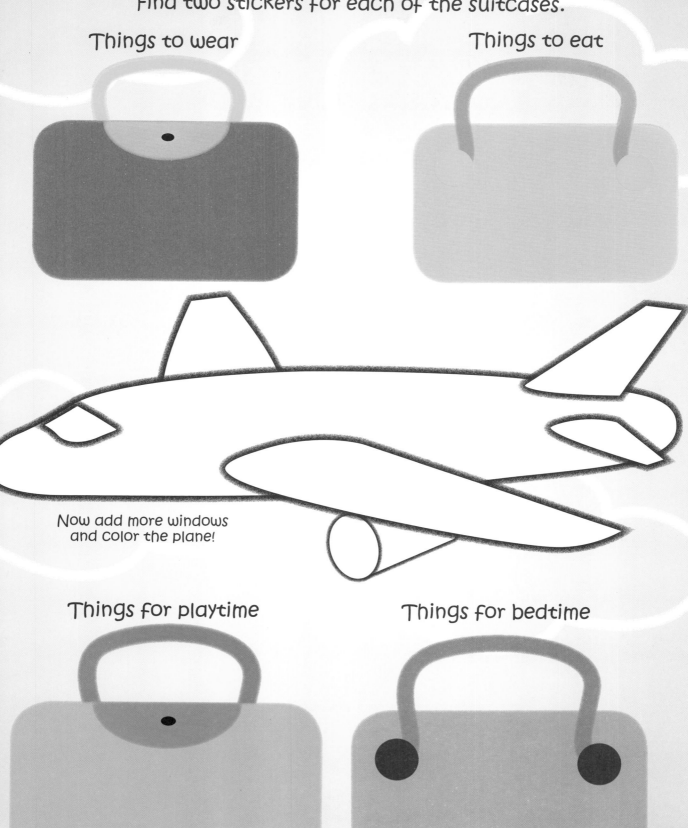

Now add more windows
and color the plane!

Things for playtime

Things for bedtime

Color your own racing car!

Connect the dots to complete the sports car, then add stripes, stickers, and your own designs!

Color the traffic lights!

Odd one out!

Match the stickers, then find the one that doesn't fit in each row of vehicles.

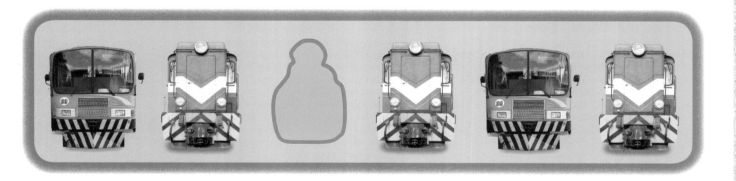

Practice drawing machines here!

38

Transportation pairs

Complete the picture with your stickers, then match the pairs with a straight line.

1) Find two sports cars.

2) Find two emergency vehicles.

3) Find two green vehicles.

4) Find two farm vehicles.

Junkyard challenge

These broken vehicles need fixing! Find the matching parts, then join them with a wiggly line.

Job List

Every time you mend a broken vehicle, find its sticker and complete the list.

Tractor

Car

Truck

Airplane

Stickers for page 2

Stickers for pages 4 & 5

Stickers for page 9

Stickers for pages 10 & 11

Stickers for pages 12 & 13

Stickers for page 14

Stickers for page 15

Stickers for pages 16 & 17

6 5 4 3 2 1